Mosaic:

Stories that Changed Our Lives

Mosaic:

Stories that Changed Our Lives

By members of the

Unitarian Universalist Church of

Urbana-Champaign, Illinois

Thanks to the contributors...

This book would not be in your hands were it not for...

- Kathy Robinson, whose editing skills made all of the difference in the way this book reads

- John Sfondilias, whose amazing photography is the ribbon that wraps this project up in a perfect cover

- Everyone who wanted to participate in this project but couldn't this time around

And to all of the authors who put up with my constant whines and reminders over the past year...

Thanks for your wealth of talent and willingness to be part of this first-time project.

In other words, you all rock!

Gail Cohen, Project Coordinator

Foreword

As the minister at UUCUC, I have the privilege of hearing stories every day: stories of perseverance, bravery, strength, humor, and mystery. I hear stories on Sunday mornings during Fellowship time, in my office over tea, and sometimes whispered at a bedside.

A few of our Worship Associates have shared stories from the pulpit, and we hear very short stories in "Joys and Sorrows" each Sunday, but mostly our stories are hidden, known only to a few friends and family.

When Gail Cohen approached me about collecting writing from people in the congregation, on the theme "the story that changed my life," I enthusiastically agreed to support the project. I suspected that the stories would be powerful, and indeed they are.

I was struck, as I read the manuscript, how many people described moments of tremendous hardship, and how it is in the midst of hardship or even tragedy that a life is transformed.

I know that it took courage and effort on the part of each person to share these stories. I know it was a labor of love for Gail to use her professional skills to run workshops, edit each person's work, and compile the essays in this book. May these stories inspire and bring us closer together as a community. Blessed be.

Reverend Florence Caplow

Introduction

What's a life-changing story? The question was bandied about endlessly as prospective authors—members of the Unitarian Universalist Church of Urbana-Champaign—tried to figure out whether they had a tale to tell during the year it took to complete this anthology.

Of course, the answer is that everybody has a life-changing story; that's the reason authors struggled hard to put words to paper. It seems the job of picking just one proved as daunting as the experiences themselves.

But somehow—thanks to persistence, kind harassment and encouragement—the mission became real. Inspiring stories from ordinary individuals who had lost loved ones, celebrated achievements and survived against all odds morphed from a series of tales to a cohesive whole.

In the end, a treasure trove of emotion, heroism, heritage and hope grew from those first seeds. Who could not be impressed by the fortitude and courage of our writers and their amazing contributions?

Did some of us struggle? You bet! But the writers whose works you will read within these pages didn't let go and they didn't give up. They worked assiduously to dig out memories, add vivid detail to their experiences, and struggle through the editing process. You are about to read their stories. Each one is a treasure.

Contents

Thanks to the contributors   i

Foreword   ii

Introduction   iii

My 82nd Year • *Sally Babbitt*   1

Have You Ever Heard a Loon Call? • *Kate Barton*   8

A Story That Changed My Life • *Jerry Carden*   10

The Little Curly-Haired Girl & Her Elders • *Beth Cobb*   17

A Road Well-Traveled • *Gail Cohen*   19

The New Normal • *Nancy Dietrich*   27

Walking Matters • *Lee Doppelt*   34

Refugee Heritage & Moral Responsibility • *Benjamin Leff*   41

Journey for Water • *Pat Nolan*   44

Cambodia 1970 • *Kathleen Robbins*   47

Insight Working • *Kathleen Robinson*   50

Summer Invasion • *Umeeta Sadarangani*   53

Safari • *Sarah Wisseman*   61

Author Biographies   68

My 82nd Year

Sally Babbitt

The appearance of an oncologist, "Dr. P P," on the cardiac ward, was a moment of stark reality. He was unknown to me, and I was not expecting to see an oncologist. Immediately, I knew he was not there to discuss the weather or my heart.

The end of October 2016, I had a CT scan for abdominal pain in the Emergency Room. I had an unexpected episode of diverticulosis. The ER MD announced there were diverticula AND there was a problem with several "masses" in various locations, probably metastasis from the radical nephrectomy done in 2003. These masses were in both lungs, left thyroid, tail of the pancreas, in the muscle near the right scapula, and a lymph node in the right retroperitoneal area.

It was assumed all these masses were metastases from the original Clear Cell Renal Carcinoma. I'd had negative ultrasound scans every year since the surgery. Nary a clue of what was lurking in the corners of my body. I went home to contemplate my fate and to imagine what the ominous future would hold for me.

Two weeks after the Emergency Room CT scan, I was watching the TV evening news when I experienced an episode of frightening panic, shortness of breath, confusion, and a pulse that was skipping beats crazily.

I called my neighbors, who arrived immediately, and we tried to call the Nurse Advisor at Carle Hospital. I described my symptoms and she put me on Hold. Meanwhile, Cara, my neighbor, called 911 for an ambulance ride (no sirens or lights). The Advisory nurse came to the phone as the ambulance was pulling into the drive.

After the medics surveyed the situation and took my vitals, they said, "Let's go." The efficient EMT started an IV, had the EKG going, and was engaging me in conversation as we sped to the emergency room and subsequent hospitalization. For several hours I was in the ER while they tried various drugs, but the Beat did *not* go on (properly).

I was rolled on my bed to the eighth floor. There I lay awake, watching the EKG line on the monitor continue to quiver, recording persistent Atrial Fibrillation, "AFib." I was *willing* my heart to resume normal sinus rhythm. At 7 a.m. the AFib resolved.

As I was "out of the woods" and my heart had calmed, since I was already in the hospital the doctors decided to biopsy with CT control the largest pulmonary lesion, which was quite close to the left ventricle of my heart. It was easily accomplished by a talented interventional radiologist.

The afternoon arrival of Dr. P.P. was to inform me that yes, indeed, the mass biopsied by frozen section was metastatic renal cell carcinoma. In that moment everything permanently changed for me. He was quoting unbelievable statics which were not good. I was considered to be a patient diagnosed with Stage 4 Cancer at multiple sites. Not a good thing.

Time to get the Living Will, THE will, the powers of attorney, and health care in order. After discharge with a new-to-me drug, Warfarin, nicely regulated, came the biopsies of other lesions: thyroid, tail of the pancreas, muscle of the scapula. All were reported as metastatic renal carcinoma, or mRCC.

The AFib medications were not working. My neighbors and I made two more trips to the ER on consecutive dates in the middle of the night. I was given IV heart medications. VERY Scary. Subsequently, when I called for an appointment, I was told my cardiologist was not available for two weeks.

I called the patient complaint office and had an appointment with an electro-physiologist the next morning at 8 a.m. He ordered two medications which controlled the AFib, but the side effects of extreme dizziness and fatigue were horrid. Of course, I was not able to speak to the doctor.

Nurse Mary fielded my complaints. I finally resolved on my own that I would try taking half the amount of the two medications. She had a very negative response to my suggestions and essentially relieved herself of any responsibility. Fortunately, the half-doses worked well.

In January 2017, I sought a second opinion at the U of Chicago Urology Oncology Department. The battery of medical student, nurse practitioner, resident/fellow, and finally THE Oncologist who specialized in mRCC told me to go home and enjoy my life, as the tumor seemed to be slow growing and "active surveillance" or "watch and wait" was what he recommended.

Hmmm. My oncologist Dr. P.P., the tumor board at Carle Hospital, and my old friend and boss, Dr. Michael Solomon, from Princeton, New Jersey, all concurred.

Watchful waiting for me follows a curve of mental gyrations. Right after the CT scan when the report is "No Change" I breathe a sigh of relief and relax—for a while. As the next scan appointment gets nearer, my anxiety level begins to rise, with a feeling that this will be the one that moves me to the next level of treatment and that death is incrementally moving closer.

I subscribe to a Physician's Update computer program that at least once a week reports on various results of clinical trials. My anxiety rises, trying to make sense of the anti-angiogenic drugs, the immunology drugs, combos of them, how toxic are they, do they really let you live 2+ more years, what are the side effects, and on and on.

Do I increase my anxiety? *Yes*. Do I make myself crazy trying to figure out the ramifications of the disease, the consequences of treatment, the ultimate outcome? *Death*. Researchers are delving into the molecular basis of RCC, genetic sequencing to find mutations and whether targeted therapy with combos of drugs can produce longer life without killing the patient.

Since that original CT scan, I have been surveilled every six months with CT scans. The radiologists have reported the findings as "No Change" until the last in mid-October 2018. The changes showed small increments of enlargement in the lung tumors and in the lymph node in the abdomen. YIKES! Now what? My complacency is shattered. Again, another event that has changed my equilibrium.

The meditation exercises, the hopeful words of my psychologist, and the wise words of my primary physician were comforting. During the last re-visit in mid-October, 2018, Dr. P.P. talked about stereotactic radiation but wanted the advice of the tumor board. His thoughts and plans were to forgo the chemotherapy treatment, as it is very toxic. My age and "co-morbidities" have to be considered.

The chemo available is very toxic and few of the preferred drugs prolong life more than months. I am told by the oncologist that the insurance companies and Medicare dictate that the "first line of therapy" must be used until it is not effective. Then perhaps the immunologic drugs can be used—that is, if you are not already dead.

However, on the bright side, 10 years ago there were NO drugs available. Sometimes there seems to be a cure with these VEGF (vascular epithelial growth factor drugs) that reportedly compromise the blood supply to tumors, but not often. On the other hand, I'm old with a gimpy heart and other physical maladies that make the available chemo a moot point of discussion.

What about the suggestion that stereotactic radiation might be possible? Watch and wait for the tumors to get bigger and therefore, make the pinpoint radiation more feasible? Why can't we call a surgeon and remove it? Again, comes the phrase back to haunt – watch and wait….enjoy your life….do whatever you desire.

To educate myself I have attended UU workshops and classes focused upon Death. Somehow after doing the fundamental paperwork I still cannot make myself think about what death will be like.

While I'm watching and waiting, the suggestion from the daughter and others to move to a senior living facility became more clamorous. I followed through and initially settled on one of the premier "old folks homes" in the area, a place offering lovely amenities, grounds, and the rooms are beautiful. It offers a continuum of care, making it the "best skilled nursing" facility in the surrounding area.

I applied and was rejected. Are you ready? I was rejected because my income projected to be inadequate to cover the cost of the "skilled nursing" care recently quoted at $8,700 per month. WOW. That and the $93,000+ admission fee was astounding.

My wonderful daughter offered to guarantee the $185,000 required from them to allow me to matriculate to THE BEST senior living place. I declined her kind offer.

The other senior facility is lovely. It has a far different financial plan. Several people I know are living there and are enjoying their lives. I'm on the waiting list for admission there.

Research and investigating the offerings for living facilities available in this geographic area makes me uneasy and uncertain. Why don't I just stay in my condo, enjoy the lake, my neighbors and the stairs to the second floor? Well, it's lonely. If I don't schedule an event the day can pass without any interaction from a single soul. My fault, yes, it probably is. Driving at night is becoming more hazardous.

Should I join more groups so that I would feel obligated to "do" something other than read, make cards, watch TV and feed the cat…who, by the way, is 20 years old and on his last legs himself. Sadly, he beat me to the big litter pan in the sky in March.

My daughter lives in Chicago in a house built in 1895, which is not conducive for more people than the three of them for happy living. Apparently, it would not be safe for me to have an apartment in the area.

The rejection of what I had envisioned as my future living arrangements is devastating. Following closely, the rejection of "the Best Senior Facility" in Champaign was equally devastating but I was able to find a great place that wanted me as much as I wanted it.

The Days of my Life are sifting through the hour glass. For want of something better which seems accepting and feasible, I am "watching and waiting" for my future to unfold. Hopefully, my funds will last as long as I do.

"Have you ever heard a loon call? It will stir your soul."
Monty Read 9/19/14

Have You Ever Heard a Loon Call?

Kate Barton

For two and a half months I followed you like a Sherpa, loaded down with the things I needed to make it through the days at your bedside. Books to read aloud to remind you of the trip you wanted to make to the Boundary Waters, a place you longed to return to. A notebook and a calendar to keep records of your surgeries, medications, and doctors. Lotion for your hands, pictures of the family whose names you could no longer say. Flowers from the garden we had planted: irises and zinnias.

Every morning I would lie in bed and try to remember where you were. From hospitals in Peoria or Urbana to the nursing home in Danville. Every evening after work I would finish calls on my cell phone at the end of the lane, collect the mail, and head into the house that had become my refuge, the place where I could try to rest and listen to the sounds of the lake.

Initially, we thought you would survive the brain hemorrhage. The girls and I sat by your bed listening to the machines and shuffling steps of doctors and nurses. After the fourth day, they showed us the shower of strokes, starlight, that had taken over your brain.

There were days when you spoke and more when you didn't, but every day we cried. Both of us cheated out of growing old together.

I kept Jess and Angelia apprised of your condition on a daily basis. Jess was wrapping up her teaching in Milwaukee and decided to move back to Illinois to help with your care. Angelia was interning in Maryland, a place we had planned to visit. It broke my heart to see them so sad. They adored you. It had always been the three of you until I came along.

The day finally came when I knew there was no more hope left. I stood alone in the ICU surrounded by medical staff who wanted to try "one more thing," I spoke for you as I had been and said that you did not want anything else done. You had become your worst nightmare: a medical invalid destined to spend the rest of whatever time you had left in a nursing home.

We brought you home. Even though you had not spoken or opened your eyes for days, you smiled when we told you that you were back in the house on the lake. Two days later in the early morning hours, I held your hand as you slipped away.

One year to the day, at the exact moment you passed, I sat in the cabin at the edge of the Boundary Waters where we had planned to travel. And as the candle I had been burning all week sputtered out, a loon started to call, and you stirred my soul.

A Story That Changed My Life

Jerry Carden

My early life found me born to a long line of farmers. My great-great-great grandparents emigrated from England in 1819 and settled in Ohio. My great-great grandparents bought land in Iowa in 1851 as part of the westward expansion. We've owned our current farm there for over 150 years. I now consider that rural Midwest background a blessing.

But that background nearly killed me. It was actually social pressure in that kind of background that almost killed me... the pressures of my local community and what I thought it meant to be a 'real' man... and the categorical thinking of society in general as to what it means to be bisexual or gay and how you should behave if in that category. I was born in 1955, so was a child of the turbulent 60s and completed high school and college in the 1970s. This was prior to the internet, and prior to my hearing about gay people at all.

My first recollection of seeing the word "homosexual" was in fifth grade—seeing the word and description in a book titled *Encyclopaedia of Sexuality*, discovered in my parents' linen closet. With a copyright of 1946, the year they were married, I assumed it to be my parent's sex manual. It was a compendium of scholarly chapters written by a variety of early sex researchers such as Kraft-Ebbing, Havelock Ellis, Freud, Jung, and others.

The chapter on homosexuality, or "*sexual inversion,*" as it was also called, wasn't totally negative about those attracted to the same gender, but it enlightened me that polite society did NOT approve. One paragraph stood out for me as an anchor to chain my hopes for transformation. It explained that it was not uncommon for pubertal and hormonal adolescents to go through a period of same-sex attraction. IF, however, that attraction hadn't gone away by age 17, the person was destined to be homosexual.

Bummer! I was getting closer and closer to that age as I read and re-read those words and that chapter. My infatuation with the male body and psyche only grew stronger as I neared that age.

Friends have often heard me refer to my childhood as being middle-of-the-road Methodist. My family attended church religiously—every OTHER Sunday. We didn't want people thinking us too pious, but also not too heathen. The Bible stories taught in Sunday School seemed the same to me as fairy tales. The creeds we were required to learn and recite in the Methodist's confirmation class during middle school years were hard for me to recite, let alone believe.

My parents were actually pretty liberal, but as I went through the painful awareness of my growing attraction toward men, I didn't feel I could talk to my parents or anyone else about why I preferred looking at naked men throwing hay bales rather than ogling buxom calendar pin-ups that hung on the walls of tractor repair shops and country taverns I frequented with my dad and his cronies.

I knew that in polite society one shouldn't talk about sex or religion. But in addition to my sexual longings, first recognized as a toddler, I felt a spiritual longing or calling. Probably in connection with the pain I felt over my deep secret. At puberty, the homosexual fantasies increased, as did a desire for some sort of spiritual or religious experience more satisfying and more exciting than Methodism.

11

Conflicted in so many ways, I relieved my childhood stress with overeating and becoming the fat and happy-on-the-outside class clown. In high school I learned that alcohol was a better stress reliever and social lubricant than gorging on snack foods. I was still trying vainly to numb the inner pain.

In the 70s, there was a religious movement called Jesus Freaks that appealed to me as a way to change and/or bury myself alive. Ready to burst or kill myself, I confided my same-sex fantasy fears to a man that I worked for during a couple summers. He persuaded me that by giving my life to Jesus and being saved, I would also be saved from my attraction to men. I was pointed toward the fundamentalist Bible church he attended.

There I also found an attraction to an associate pastor that I eventually appealed to for counseling. I found him somewhat attentive to me and hoped for more than counseling. I did countless altar calls and professed several salvations through Jesus--sometimes for the benefit of Pastor Bill's admiration. I pretty much knew the prayers were in vain, as my desires got stronger.

No amount of praying or counseling sessions with Pastor Bill relieved me of my preference for looking at the guys in the locker room rather than buxom pinup pictures. My high school years became a chameleon existence of drinking lots of beer with friends on Friday and Saturday nights; then professing my love for Jesus on Sundays at the fundamentalist Bible church. I had reached that age of 17 mentioned in the book on sexuality.

I was feeling pretty desperate at one of my Sunday afternoon counseling and prayer sessions with Pastor Bill.

He essentially told me I wasn't praying hard enough—it was my fault, not God's.

I had often pondered whether I should snuff out my desires (and myself) so no one would ever learn my secret. I decided to let God decide my fate with a session of Russian roulette using my brother's revolver, which I was pretty sure he kept loaded. Steve was 4 years older than me, in college, but living back home that summer. He kept his gun in its holster, on the banister of the stairwell.

With gun in mouth, I stood partially hanging over the banister so the weight of my body would provide a fall hard enough to assure my intent if the gunshot didn't. My prayer to God was that if it's okay to be gay, the next chamber will be empty. It obviously was, and I also took it as a sign that it WAS okay to be gay--but I was incredibly shaken by what could have happened. I've been close to death several times since, but not by my own hand.

I was born the day before Thanksgiving, and each year as my birthday either falls near or on that holiday, I am always extra thankful to be alive.

Fast forward to college, which included summer construction jobs with sweaty, bare-chested men, and a chance to experiment with both genders—which pretty much identified me as bisexual, at about a 4.5 on the Kinsey Scale. I also joked that I'd given up both middle-of-the-road Methodism AND fundamental religion for the church of the open bottle.

My coping mechanism, and I don't recommend it, was a growing alcohol dependence and a lot of party-hearty behavior. It was the mid-70s, gay liberation was in full swing, and it was pre-AIDS. I had low self-esteem coupled with a high libido. Despite working toward a degree in health education, my unwavering belief in anything spiritual was dying with my descent into alcoholism.

I had fallen prey to the societal image as to what it meant to be a gay man. I blindly followed that stereotype displayed in media images, even though I was not comfortable with that way of living. I'd not yet met gay people that did NOT fit the stereotypes.

In 1978 I accidentally came out to my farmer brother Steve as we were both in a pretty drunken state of sharing about our lives. He was immediately supportive and encouraged me to come out to our parents. I was dubious, but then chose to write my folks a letter.

My dad came around faster than my mom, owing to his knowledge of "people like me" in his WWII years in the Navy. They both eventually became very supportive, causing my earlier fears of rejection to be unfounded. But I was still drinking—a LOT! My mother had not yet disclosed that her father was an alcoholic.

A series of experiences, including a 5-year-long, rocky relationship with an alcoholic professor, eleven years my senior, brought me to the doors of recovery in 1980.

After six months of tortured, sporadic sobriety, my actual sobriety date became July 12, 1981. I also met my current husband who gave me the courage to attend my first 12-step meeting and get out of the co-dependent relationship with the professor.

I learned in the 12-Step program I could put aside the God and religion I was steeped in and develop a belief in a higher power that made sense to me. My belief in a higher power centers around the forces of energy and a conception of a collective consciousness that exists in all living and inert things if we allow ourselves to be cognizant and aware of it.

I grew my spiritual program in recovery circles and was a regular there for about 17 years. Had I not sobered up in 1981, the first year we learned of the disease affecting gay men, later to be defined as HIV/AIDS, I know I would be dead now. My sexual behaviors prior to my sobriety date would have likely led to my demise.

The mid-1980s raised more spiritual questions as I witnessed the severe suffering and death of close friends due to AIDS and/or alcoholism. In January and July of 1991, I lost two of my closest friends (both named Steven) to AIDS.

In September of that same year, the suicide of my brother Steven led to another series of questions about the meaning of life. He did it with our dad's shotgun, even though he had plenty of his own guns in a cabinet right next to the sofa where he ended his life. Visions of my earlier attempt with Steve's revolver haunted me. How could he have actually gone through with it? How could I have attempted it so many years earlier?

These emotional trials led me to discussions about things spiritual and theological. I was told by several confidants after telling my story and my beliefs, that my views are very Unitarian-Universalist. I eventually made it to the UU Church of Urbana-Champaign. My belief in a higher power persists as the energy field that supports all life, and also some sort of universal consciousness or spirit world.

My beliefs take twists and turns as I read, meditate and discuss with others. I mostly define my beliefs as Buddhist, also honoring the Pagan cycle of the seasons, and trying to live according to the behaviors exemplified by Jesus (I am a "small-c Christian").

The institutionalized societal attitudes and stereotypes of gay persons were responsible for my feelings of alienation from society as I was growing up. That misery led me to attempted suicide and to actual alcoholism.

I'm forever grateful that in the UU fold I found not only acceptance, but true affirmation with a diverse group of like-minded people. It is through friends such as those in UU, through music—singing, piano and trombone; writing, gardening, cooking and too many hobbies; and making time for meditation that I find continual renewal.

The Little Curly-Haired Girl and Her Elders

Beth Cobb

This piece is the text of a presentation by Beth to the congregation as she prepared to retire from her church job.

Once upon a time, not so very long ago, there was little curly-haired girl who lived in a small city in the Midwest. She was a rather shy little girl who would rather read library books than go outside to ride her bike.

Every Sunday she went to church school and learned about all kinds of things—Bible stories, the wonder of nature, gods and goddesses, the importance of trying to make a difference in the world. She sang in the Junior Choir on Sunday mornings and for Christmas Eve candlelight services. A wise woman named Carolyn often led her in Children's Worship.

Years passed and she wasn't a little girl anymore, but a young woman. She began to serve her church in many ways, as a religious education (RE) leader and then as the Director of Religious Education. She learned that in order to help children with their search for truth and meaning, she needed to continue on her own search.

She got married and soon had a little curly-haired boy and a little curly-haired girl. As they will do, many people offered advice on how to care for and rear these children. The curly-haired woman listened to her elders, but the most helpful words were supportive and came from Kimi, who said, "The hardest part is making decisions every day."

And the words of Julia were also helpful. Julia asked, "And what nicknames do you have for this baby boy?" When Julia heard all of them, she said that was good. "A child with a lot of nicknames is a well-loved child."

As the curly-haired woman strove to meet the challenges of being a good wife, mother, and earning money, she often made mistakes. A very wise woman named Jane gave her some very important words: "Forgive yourself and go on." Although Jane is no longer with us, her artwork often shines upon us when we are in this room.

One bitterly cold winter morning, as the curly-haired woman was walking into church, a very wise man named Don said, "These mornings are perfect, the air is never so clear as it is on a cold morning." The curly-haired woman was reminded to appreciate all the wonders of nature and to enjoy the moment she was in.

Although the wise man Don is only in our hearts now, the woman remembers him every cold winter morning and thinks of his telling of going to church in wagons on winter mornings in Minnesota. Even if the weather is difficult, it's important to go to church.

Some more years passed and now the curly-haired woman has reached her own elder years. More and more of her elders are with her now only in her heart. She is grateful for their words of wisdom.

She remembers well that those of us who are still living here are charged with carrying on their ministry in the world. She makes an effort to greet newcomers with the hospitality of Judy, to bring and serve food as Florence always did, and to dress up for an occasion, remembering Florence saying that doing so acknowledges that it is a special moment.

And she tries to pass on her own words of wisdom to the young ones.

A Road Well-Traveled

Gail Cohen

As folks living in Chicago can attest, weather can be perfect one minute and disastrous the next. When snow and winds aren't pummeling Lake Michigan's shore and bedroom communities, tornadoes unceremoniously drop in from the south.

Enduring dramatic weather change becomes a badge of honor for those happy to swap the lifestyle and magic of Chicago for towns and cities in areas with fewer perks, but fate brought us to Chicago and that was that. So, when faced with the job of organizing a road trip from Chicago to Georgia during the "iffy season," I admit to being less than thrilled.

If I had my druthers, I'd have flown the friendly skies to Atlanta, but my husband and I were recovering from our late-in-life adventure: we had quit our jobs to pursue graduate degrees. Four years later, we were a couple of the most well-educated paupers on the planet.

Further, the trip to Georgia was mandated. I had been summoned to the offices of the anthropology department at the University of Georgia to face a firing squad summarily known as "the oral defense."

Sound like a dental procedure? Close. Only nobody would give me Novocain before I sat for hours trying to prove that I've amassed enough data to prove why female suicide in pre-revolutionary China was rampant. I admit to trepidation as our departure loomed.

Of mandarins, mileage and melancholy

Before I could discuss mandarins, missionaries and mutilation with my committee, there was that pesky road trip for four that would take place within the confines of our well-seasoned Toyota—a little yellow vehicle, old in the tooth, but reliable and no less worthy of our confidence as we made plans.

I'm obsessive. No apologies. My mind climbed the Everest of things that could go wrong on our drive south. *Car checked out by a mechanic?* Done. *Motor club contacted?* You bet. In this pre-GPS era, I trudged to the AAA office to claim packets of road maps prepared for our journey south.

To my kids' chagrin and dismay, we informed them that this would be "a rocket ride," which is why the car would be stocked with food. *Yes,* to bathroom breaks. *No* to burger breaks. They were none too pleased.

In some respect, I felt sorry for my kids, saddled as they were with graduate-student parents chasing late-in-life dreams that left them the long-suffering victims. But we had a car to pack. And a departure date pending.

We hit the road. Sorta.

What little space wasn't taken up by kids in the back seat was filled with food that would allow us to drive straight through to Athens. We left late in the day to out-distance a snowstorm flirting with local weathermen, figuring we could hightail it out of the Land of Lincoln before the front blew in.

So much for the "best laid plans." The front kicked in with wild abandon and our car died on a dark road so close to the Kentucky border, I could almost smell the Bourbon and horse manure.

We were parked on the side of the road as snow fell in torrents. We looked at each other. Michael got out and raised the hood. I had no idea why. He knew as much about cars as I did—two brainiacs were we, more interested in Borneo mating rituals (me) and Keynesian economic theories (him) than how to diagnose an engine.

Yet Michael applied due diligence to his mission by putting up the hood of his parka and staring thoughtfully into the engine using the flashlight freshly stocked with batteries. In the back seat, the kids did what kids do: added to the audio tape accompanying our layover.

"I gotta go to the bathroom."

"I'm still hungry."

"Are we almost there?"

"Mom, I really have to go to the bathroom."

A coffee can was disbursed, but my daughter turned up her nose at the thought of pulling down her pants behind the car in the dark, so high drama flowed from her petulant lips. Inside the car, windows quickly iced with thin sheets of frost as temperatures dropped faster than our spirits.

Sitting in the stillness of the night on that lonely road was a torturous experience and I lay claim to the worst angst of all: my meeting with the faculty was 36 hours away and we had yet to cross a state line.

We debated the merits of staying put versus going in search of help. But Michael and I had read too many stories about highway marauders with chainsaws to give that option more than lip service. We opted to stay put and open the window only if a uniformed body appeared and was willing to shove credentials through the crack.

Not that anyone stopped, mind you. The few cars that passed raced by like bullet trains. I believe their instincts could best be summed up as, "What kind of crazy people go out in weather like this? Surely not people we would be comfortable stopping to assist."

Cell phones? I remind you of the year, gentle reader. Back then, "blackberries" described summer fruit.

As we pinned our dwindling hopes on highway patrol officials, hours crawled by. The kids fell asleep. I tried to stay calm, but my level of anxiety grew increasingly, reaching near panic stage from time-to-time.

I was being selfish, of course. I wanted that diploma and I believe that I was about to have a meaningful pre-scream breakdown when God took pity upon us. Headlights appeared in our rear window. A vehicle came to rest behind our rear bumper. A car door slammed; a shadow approached.

The man at our window had a soothing voice and understood our reticence to open windows more than a crack. Truth be told, we couldn't have identified Elvis in costume had he stood there. We were calmed by his willingness to shove his driver's license through the window, walking away as we examined it.

When he returned, he carried chocolate chip and oatmeal granola bars. *Marauders don't carry granola bars!* We opened the door.

What transpired after we agreed to take up the offer of help from this kind stranger is the stuff of which movie scripts are made. Once we were bundled inside the Samaritan's van, our rescuer explained that he was a youth minister, living in a nearby town. He and his wife were out on a mundane errand that they normally would have put off until the storm had passed.

Offering profuse words of gratitude—we must have been effusive because he insisted that we stop thanking him—he headed for the front of our car, poked around with a flashlight, and informed us that the new points I'd had installed two days earlier were faulty.

"We're going to have to find points," he declared, putting his vehicle into gear and off we went—six of us on a mini-tour of filling stations in the vicinity. After passing a few, the reverend suddenly jammed on the brakes and made a beeline for a dark, apparently unattended filling station worthy of the "Blair Witchcraft Project."

We looked out. No visible signs of life. To our astonishment, the Rev got out of his van and began throwing snowballs at second story windows above the station. A light popped on. A head appeared and pulled up the window sash. But instead of lambasting us for interrupting his sleep, the man in the PJs waved merrily and said he'd be right down.

There was much gesturing and discussion between the three men before the guys disappeared into the recesses of the shop. Returning like Magi laden with toolboxes and cardboard cartons, they loaded them into the van, and off we went to find the telltale mound of snow that was our car, parked on the easement of the highway.

"We've got everything we need to get you fixed up," said the reverend, whose name I'm ashamed to have forgotten. "Won't take but a few minutes to get your car running," he said, looking into my eyes in the rearview mirror from his perch behind the wheel.

I know you want to ask the question, dear reader: How does a rural gas station, with what didn't appear to be a state-of-the-art repair shop, happen to stock points for the old Toyota we drove? Well, the answer is that I'm clueless. Lots of book learning. Short on faith. The items we needed to move forward just appeared. While Michael observed, tools flew as we sat in the safe cocoon of the van.

They say that hearing a baby's cry for the first time is unforgettable. In my opinion, my engine turning over that night surpassed any sound a newborn could make—even if that child happened to come from my womb. The couple begged us to stay the night with them, but I had an appointment with destiny that he had helped make happen, and so we ruefully turned down the offer of warm beds.

Like Robert Frost, we had miles to go before we slept…

…and, in my case, hours to go before my thesis committee would challenge every last one of my brain cells to find out if I really knew more than most about why women committed suicide in China. With warm hugs and handshakes, the reverend and his wife graciously bid us goodbye, refusing to take cash, just as the service station owner we had awakened wouldn't take anything more from us than the cost of the parts needed to repair the car.

To be certain that we were in no imminent danger of breaking down again, our saviors followed us down the highway a bit. When last we saw them, they were steering toward an exit ramp. I recognized it as the one leading to the service station that was the source of our manna from heaven. Our wandering road saint was heading back to return everything he had borrowed.

"Incredulous" doesn't begin to describe feelings I experienced when we were again on the road driving south. I'm a New York City girl who's skeptical about strangers who claim not to have motives. Until then, I had never met a person who went out of his way to help just because it was the right thing to do. Selflessness does not compute in a brain that's hard wired for sarcasm, flip retorts and irony.

And yet I could not deny the reality of what had happened. And so, I learned about the meaning of goodness that night as all four of us took that goodwill with us as we raced south to meet my deadline.

The sun had risen when we pulled into the driveway of friends who had expected us for hours and were worried that we had been in an accident. Our story came out jumbled. There was just enough time to get the kids settled into beds while I grabbed a shower and prayed I would neither start babbling nor pass out during what I knew would be the arduous grilling awaiting me in an hour.

Thankfully, extreme fatigue left me incapable of freaking out and either over-talking my oral defense or saying too little to convince those scrutinizing scholars that I deserved to pass muster. The torture lasted nearly three hours and when I stood, my knees literally buckled. But I passed with distinction, despite being disoriented and exhausted.

I'm happy to report that our drive home was incident-free, and while decades have passed—husbands have come and gone; grandchildren grown up and great-grandchildren popping up like dandelions—when I am alone in my car in the solitude known only to night-driving motorists—memories flooding my brain are as fresh today as they were back then.

When heavy snow falls over a desolate road in the midst of nowhere, I'm back there on that highway on my way to Georgia. Feeling vulnerable. Frightened. Until the face of a stranger with mechanical skills and friends in high places appears—a guy with no intention of going out into a snowstorm or of finding a service station stocked with tools and parts needed to repair an old Japanese car for a bunch of strangers heading south.

The New Normal

Nancy Dietrich

When I woke up in the recovery room after my operation on July 17, 2017 and overheard the nurse saying, "She had a full hysterectomy," I knew my life had changed forever. You see, I wasn't going to have a full hysterectomy unless the pathology report came back malignant. So that's how I found out I had ovarian cancer.

I learned more details once I was moved to my own room: my cancer was caught at Stage 1A, the earliest stage. But my surgeon was awaiting a consultation with Mayo Clinic to get more details on the specific cell type. That took two more weeks. The results: Clear Cell Carcinoma, a rare cell type that is always considered Grade 3, according to my surgeon. Grade 3 is described online as "cancer cells that look abnormal and may grow or spread more aggressively." My surgeon, Dr. K, recommended six cycles of chemotherapy. Now, at 45 years old, I was officially a cancer patient.

Two months before, I had been gaining weight and finding that, in my 40s, the weight wasn't coming off as easily as it used to. My husband Russ and I had laughed that I kind of looked pregnant, and I joked, "maybe I have a huge tumor in my gut." As someone who enjoys a nice craft beer or a glass of wine in the evening, I decided to cut down to only on weekends or a special occasion. Maybe that would help reduce the "beer gut."

One day in the middle of June I got on the scale at my gym and was shocked to find that I was tipping the scales at a weight I'd never been before. That was the first time it dawned on me that something really might be wrong. With exercising and my current reasonable diet, there was no way I should have been gaining that kind of weight. So I made an appointment with my primary doctor, who felt the mass and immediately started the ball rolling with a visit to the gynecologist, scans, an appointment with the area's only gynecologic-oncologist—my surgeon, Dr. K at Carle Clinic (who I liked and trusted implicitly from the get-go)—and a date scheduled for surgery, all in a matter of two weeks.

Dr. K told me there was a decent chance it wasn't cancer, but he wouldn't know until surgery, where they removed the mass and sent it to pathology. Later, he told me they were surprised, after removing it, that the tumor ended up being cancerous.

There were three main reasons the cancer diagnosis was such a shock to me. First, I had a cancer scare eight years earlier when, at age 38, a tumor was found in my left eye. I had one of the best doctors in the country at Barnes Jewish Hospital in St. Louis for that one. He was confident the tumor was not malignant, so we watched and waited a year before treating it. This type of eye tumor, depending on the type, can be very aggressive (sound familiar?).

But eight years later, there was no sign of metastasis. Surely one cancer scare was enough to last me at least three or four decades, I thought. The second reason it was such a shock is that I come from a fairly large family, and no family member that I know of has had any type of cancer. Third reason: I could be the poster child for "doing everything right." I've always been physically active, never been overweight, try to eat organic food when possible, and since the eye cancer scare eight years before, I've made kale smoothies almost religiously five days a week. I thought I was off the hook, until I heard those words from the nurse in the recovery room.

I was determined to get as much information as possible about my newly-discovered disease, so I started by searching online: "Stage 1A Clear Cell Carcinoma of the Ovary." I liked typing in "Stage 1A" before the rest of the diagnosis; it made the diagnosis feel more manageable. So, what did I find out through my research on the Internet? Some good news, actually. Several studies showed that Stage 1A Clear Cell has a good, if not excellent, prognosis, especially if one has negative cytology (no cancer cells in the abdominal washings). Yes—that's me!

In fact, a couple of studies remarked that chemotherapy may not even be needed for Stage 1A CC. I also found one study in which the findings showed that six cycles of chemotherapy were no more effective for Clear Cell than three cycles.

Armed with this good news, I consulted with Dr. K about doing three cycles, but he still recommended six. And he wouldn't be the doctor overseeing the chemotherapy; I'd have to go to another oncologist. Although I respected his opinion highly, I decided to get a second opinion, and it meant a lot to me that I had his blessing—Dr. K highly recommended the gynecologic/oncology department at Barnes Jewish Hospital in St. Louis, where I had had a positive experience with my eye treatments previously.

I immediately felt comfortable with Dr. P, the head of gynecologic oncology at Barnes. "You're asking the right questions," he remarked as I went through the list of research papers I had consulted. He confirmed what I was reading: the findings seem to show little added benefit to chemotherapy, but it's hard to tell people *not* to go through it because, he said, "People die from this."

But he added, "You need to do what will make you sleep at night." His honesty with me about my situation made me realize that, if I decided to go through chemotherapy, this was where I was going to get it done, with Dr. P as the supervising oncologist.

But it was an agonizing decision to make: Either go through chemotherapy with its numerous potential long-term side effects, or not go through it and risk recurrence with the side effect of regret for not doing everything I could have done to prevent the cancer from returning.

And in the case of Clear Cell, recurrence is extremely difficult to treat. I received a third opinion from Mayo Clinic, and their recommendation was also chemotherapy. I decided I would undergo three cycles because, as Dr. P suggested, I knew it would help me sleep at night knowing I had done everything I could to prevent recurrence.

On Sept. 5, 2017 I started three cycles of chemotherapy at Barnes in St. Louis, scheduled once a week for nine weeks (one cycle = three weeks of treatment). I found an extended-stay hotel in the St. Louis area that was relatively affordable and made reservations. That place became a home away from home for the next two months.

The first day was a whirlwind of activity: surgery to get my port placed, followed immediately by chemotherapy that afternoon. We ended up staying the entire week in St. Louis that first week between treatments because I was having some concerns about my port, in addition to having an allergic skin reaction to one of the chemotherapy drugs. I was so grateful to have a comfortable, homey place to stay while I was going through treatment.

As expected, I started losing my hair about three treatments in. I didn't think it would affect me that much, but it did. I had a hard time looking at myself in the mirror. I ordered a couple of baseball caps designed for hair loss and that was my main "look" as I went through treatment. I also wore a wig that I already had (that's a story for another time), for special occasions. I guess losing my hair was difficult because it was a constant reminder that I had cancer.

The two months I went through chemotherapy were difficult for me emotionally. I experienced the extreme fatigue common with treatment, but because of the allergic skin reaction I had, I was also on large doses of steroids which sometimes made me feel like I was going crazy. A fellow ovarian cancer survivor told me, "Try not to personalize it too much. Chemotherapy doesn't define who you are." Such simple but good advice. I thought of that each time I went through treatment

My husband, Russ, has been my rock throughout this entire experience. I don't know what I would do without him. He is the one who has made me feel like everything will be OK, in the calm, reassuring way that he has. When Russ couldn't go to St. Louis with me for treatment on a couple of occasions, my mom accompanied me. At first, I wasn't sure if this would be a good idea because I felt like I would have to be strong for her, instead of the other way around. But she was much stronger than I anticipated. I have spent more than one night crying on her shoulder. I don't know what I'd do without her, either.

Here are some musings I've had about living with cancer:

- Right now, I live in 3-month increments: the time between my follow-up appointments. The first couple of months seem almost normal; then the last month the anxiety starts to creep in. I hope it gets easier.

- Many cancer survivors find strength through "warrior" language: "Battling cancer;" "Kicking cancer's ass;" etc. Online support groups use the term "teal warriors" (teal is the "color" for ovarian cancer). I understand why it might be helpful for some people, but I haven't been able to embrace it. I'm not sure if there is such a thing as helpful language when it comes to cancer.

- Even though I've been through cancer treatment, I don't always know what to say to other people who have had cancer. So, I don't expect anyone to know what to say to me. I think it's more important to say or do something to show that you care, rather than worrying about how it comes across and not say anything at all.

- I definitely think my cancer has environmental causes. There is very little research money spent on figuring out the environmental causes of cancer. This needs to change, but I'm not sure how to help bring that about.

- Because my husband and I are self-employed, we purchase our health insurance on the national exchange, thanks to the ACA. I support Medicare for All, but in its absence, I am very grateful for the ACA, as it has made health insurance more affordable for us. I worry about whether the ACA will be around much longer, if the Republicans continue to chip away at it. I'm a perfect example of why everyone needs health insurance, even if you're relatively young and healthy. I hope to see the day when health care in this country is understood to be a basic human right.

- I have never been angry about getting cancer; just sad and scared. I'm still scared. While I have a reasonably good prognosis, some days it's hard to stay positive.

I've thought a lot about death since my diagnosis. Having cancer has forced me to face my mortality in a way I haven't had to before. I'm afraid of dying. I am seeing a spiritual counselor who is helping me sort through my fears. I've started reading books that talk about death and dying from a spiritual perspective to help me deal with these feelings.

Meditation and mindfulness classes have helped, too. But I'm still afraid. I hope to come to a point of peace and acceptance about death, but I'm not there yet. I would never say that cancer is a gift. But cancer has taught me that life is short. None of us knows how long we will live, so each of us has to find what is truly important to give our lives meaning and try to live that out each and every day. This is my new normal.

Walking Matters

Lee Doppelt

Walking has changed my life.

Approximately 10 years ago, I terminated my pool-gym membership after 25 years, opting for a more flexible and cheaper exercise plan.

Approaching middle age, I pursued a program with aerobic exercise to get my heart pumping, and weight-bearing activity to strengthen hip bones. Also, subject to unexplained sadness on gloomy days, especially during autumn and winter, I also wanted activity that brought me outdoors in warm or cold weather, for exposure to natural light and sunshine to ramp up my Vitamin D levels naturally.

The obvious solution presented itself to me when my friend, who I will call "Darlene," asked me to go walking. We walked outdoors nearly 60 minutes around my neighborhood and talked about everything—from upcoming weekend plans to issues with adult children and grandchildren. The walk was invigorating to my body, therapeutic, and also calming to my often restless spirit. Darlene and I walked daily for months—outdoors, or indoors during inclement weather.

We still get together for walks, though less frequently, as our schedules are sometimes out of sync. Darlene has been the friend who's listened to my ideas, some solid and some whacky. And though she's supportive and positive, she keeps me honest, and challenges things I say that don't resonate well.

I like having an older friend like Darlene who's very smart, comfortable in her own skin, and has wisdom and perspective. I admire and respect her. Perhaps spending enough time with Darlene, I'll become more like her!

There are many people who've surfaced as walking pals. And I've joined some walking groups that collectively walk as often as four times weekly, outdoors in all seasons and temperatures. These people are heartier than average.

Conversations with these folks are highly dependent on who's in the group. Typically, in larger groups people splinter off with others who walk at approximately the same speed, and conversation is arbitrary, based on how many are in the smaller group (often 2 to 4 people) and how well they know each other, but usually conversation is superficial with topics such as which state park is loveliest this time of year, or where to get a sofa reupholstered.

Conversations when walking with male friends are often focused on topics like the best way to get a bicycle tune-up, or how to keep the house crawl space moisture-free. The conversations on one-to-one walks with woman friends tend to be more "up close and personal" as they say, especially as the frequency of walks increases and we get to know each other better.

"Jill" is a bit younger than me, but much to my initial surprise, her stamina for walking is less than mine, as is her tolerance for weather. If it seems too warm or too cool outside, she'd rather be indoors reading a good book. But when she's up for walking, she's a true joy. She has a strong spiritual side and solid value system. And she's one of those people who is so open-minded and always sees the good in people. No gossip when Jill is present!

I pride myself in having very high standards on just about everything, but the downside of that is that I often find myself being too judgmental and negative about people. If I could be more like Jill, I'd truly be a better person.

"Alex" is a new friend; being in a similar line of work is what brought us together, and we often talk about work-related situations and help each other find practical solutions. People tell me that I have lots of energy, but clearly Alex, who's an athlete, has me beat.

I have some wild pie-in-the-sky ideas at times, especially when it comes to projects, such as things I might like to write about, and she helps nourish those ideas and makes me think bigger and bigger. I like that Alex helps keep the dreamy side in me alive. I wish we could find more time for our early morning walks. I miss you, Alex!

"Lucy" is an occasional walking pal, and also much younger than me. Like all my walking friends, she's in a good marriage with a husband but also has young school-aged children for whom she cooks a big breakfast each morning. So, I drive to her house before the crack of dawn and she sneaks out so we can take a long walk around her neighborhood. I don't think her family has a clue she's been out walking while they were all still asleep.

Lucy is an artisan, making customized religious tapestries and other self-designed handmade goods, which she sells via her website and at boutique art fairs. She knows that I have had one business or another since age 13 and she often bounces business ideas off of me.

I was surprised when she called me last night with some questions about how to price certain items that she was selling. I like that I can be helpful to Lucy, but I admire her energy and sense of conviction to her craft. She inspires me to do more, and to be more creative.

"Cindy" is a friend from work. She's very active in her church and is my idea of what it takes to be "a good Christian." She's truly a good person. She is quiet, she is calm, she is gentle, she is kind; but if I say something negative, I can feel the vibe that I need to shape up or shut up. We talk a lot about work-related issues, good and bad, and much about our families, including having aging parents. Cindy is my role model for just being good.

Though "Maureen" and I went to college together and lived in the same dorm, we didn't really connect until the mid-1990s, under circumstances that are best left for writing the next story that changed my life. I remember Maureen from back in the early 1970s because she was the first person I ever saw in a wheelchair.

It wasn't so much that I was clueless, though in many ways I was, but that legislation for people with disabilities was several years away from being written; people with disabilities had few rights or opportunities and were therefore essentially "invisible" members of society.

Maureen had used a wheelchair her entire life. And ironically in the past few years, she's become one of my favorite walking buddies. I cannot keep up with the speed of Maureen's motorized wheelchair, so she keeps me going in more ways than I've expressed to her. Maureen never lets herself be a victim. She's more empowered than many of my ambulatory friends and has learned well how to travel locally on city busses as well as on vacations around the country. I always appreciate all that I have when I'm around Maureen. Thank you, Maureen, for "walking" with me.

A newer walking friend is "Brenda." I met her at a dinner a few years back. She's much younger than I am and has a lot of fire and passion in her. Yes, I remember being like that not so many years ago. Her stamina for walking is great, so she is becoming one of my favorite walking buddies.

Brenda is a cancer survivor. She takes really good care of herself, and knows of no cancer in her family, so her cancer came as a total shock. But she got through it. Today, on our walk at beautiful nearby Mattis Park, this crisp autumn morning with the leaves turning colors, she shared with me the most devastating part of having cancer; hair loss from chemotherapy. Brenda admits to not being particularly vain, but losing her hair made her feel old, she says, and made it hard to keep her cancer a secret.

I am not at all vain, but still, I freak out when I find loose hair of mine in my hairbrush or on my pillow. I researched hair loss in middle-aged women and was put at ease to learn that we each lose 50 to 100 hairs every day. I still have a fairly thick mop of salt and pepper hair, but to think of losing all of it—and all at once—as Brenda did has got to be dehumanizing and screams to the world "I have cancer."

In our few walks together so far, I have learned so much from Brenda about what is important in life. And whatever is happening in my own life that may have me in a funk—the clothes dryer not working right, a cranky neighbor person in the supermarket line—pales in comparison to

what Brenda has gone through, and though she is now cancer-free, she has the cloud looming of a possible recurrence. Yes, thanks Brenda, for helping me sort out what is important.

Maybe I've learned the most from "Ginnie." She's an older woman who helped me with some personal issues around 35 years ago. Woops, I guess we never went for a walk together. But we did meet for lunch recently and I made a point of reminding her how she had helped me so many years ago and thanked her one more time.

Ginnie appears to suffer from depression. She has some serious health problems and spends a large percentage of her time at medical appointments. I, the cheerleader to all, gave her my usual pep talk to get out and do more fun things. Be active. Be busy.

She then snapped at me. "Not all of us can do so many things, and it is just frustrating to have people like you tell me to get out of the house and be busy, because I simply can't." Ginnie, of course, was correct. I was totally out of line as I often am. In my effort to be supportive and positive, I was simply reminding her of the things she couldn't do.

I swallowed my pride and apologized to Ginnie. In that short lunch (we didn't even order the free pie!), she taught me a very valuable lesson. I was looking at her situation through *my* eyes and was blind to how life must feel *to her*, someone who was formerly active and very engaged in life, but was no longer physically able to do so many things she would have wanted to do.

Ginnie probably will never become anyone's walking buddy, though I suspect she wishes she could. But she is on my list of people to call to go to lunch.

As a person who claims to be very private, I shared with the editor of this anthology, very early after its inception, that though I was, in fact, a professional writer, I wasn't used to writing from the first person point of view. After all, following my retirement, I fell into the life of writing for magazines.

I write practical stuff for print and online venues, many related to do-it-yourself house and shopping topics, such as how to purchase a refrigerator, or one of my favorite articles, "Dumpster Diving with Panache." I have written other types of articles for magazines, including over a dozen travel articles with photos, but always from the third person point of view.

Some of my walking pals have only me as their walking buddy, but I have grown to have many treasured walking friends. I feel blessed to have several blossoming friendships based on getting outside in the fresh air and being active.

It seems that my story is just other peoples' stories retold by me. But, in reality, aren't we all connected? That Brenda has had cancer has become part of my story. That Ginnie suffers from depression also touches me deeply, especially having known her as a younger, more vital woman.

Taking long walks with friends is the best! It's made me a softer, kinder, more tolerant and understanding person, I hope. So, do come walk with me, because walking matters.

For now, this is *a* story that has changed my life.

Refugee Heritage and Moral Responsibility

Benjamin Leff

One of my most cherished possessions is the passport that belonged to the family of my grandmother, Melitta Jerech, because of the story it tells. It includes the names of her parents, Heinrich and Henrietta. He was a cantor and she was a doctor.

But it also includes the names "Israel" and "Sara," which were squeezed onto the passport in 1939. Apparently at that time, these names were assigned on official documents to lots of people to clearly identify them as Jews. To remove any ambiguity, the passport also has the infamous "J" stamp, which stood for *Jude*—Jew.

As you might have deduced, I am not describing an American passport. It is labeled "Deutches Reich—Reisepass," and it features the Nazi Swastika. Melitta and her parents lived in Austria, which was annexed by Nazi Germany in 1938.

By the end of that year, they had lived through the anti-Jewish rioting of Kristallnacht, and Heinrich was one of about 300 Jews in the city of Graz who were sent to Dachau, the infamous concentration camp. The story passed down to me was that Henrietta regularly visited the Nazi commander's office until she finally managed to get a meeting and somehow persuaded him to release Heinrich.

If you turn the pages of the passport, you get to the next part of the story. There is a "Sverige" stamp showing that Melitta and her parents were accepted by Sweden in 1939—

crucially allowing them to leave Austria. They stayed in Sweden until 1940, but by then, the Nazis appeared poised to invade Northern Europe. Thus, my family sought to leave Scandinavia to find safety, making the next pages of the passport the most important at all.

It doesn't look special. It's basically bureaucratic paperwork filled out by an official at the US consulate in Stockholm. But it was life-changing and perhaps even life-saving for my 15-year-old grandmother. It was an immigration visa, granting Melitta and her parents permission to enter the United States.

In early April 1940, my family left Sweden for Norway, and boarded a ship which left Norway for America on April 7, 1940. I mention that date, April 7, because the Nazis invaded Norway on April 9. The boat even received a radio transmission saying the Nazis had invaded, but the captain chose to continue towards America.

It is impossible to know what would have happened if they had been stuck in Norway. I do know that a lot of Jews remaining in Norway were killed in the Holocaust. That could have included my grandmother and her parents if they hadn't had the stamp admitting them to the US.

It's worth noting that not all European Jews got a visa to America. Tens of thousands of Jews who applied for entry were turned away at US embassies. The Roosevelt Administration and the US Congress resisted calls to admit more Jews fleeing from Europe. In 1939, a boatload of more than 900 Jewish refugees was turned away from the coast of Florida. The ship eventually returned to Europe, and while some Jews found refuge in countries like Great Britain, more than 200 of them died in the Holocaust.

Why didn't the United States do more to help these refugees? There was certainly some plain old anti-Semitism, as some Americans wanted *fewer* Jews in America, not more. But it was also a time when war was brewing throughout the world. Many Americans, including key members of the Roosevelt Administration, feared that Jewish refugees could be Nazi spies in disguise, or that these Jews could easily be blackmailed by the Nazis into committing espionage against the US—after all, the Nazis held their families hostage.

Therefore, my grandmother and her parents were some of the lucky people who were admitted into the United States, but thousands and thousands were not. I don't know why my family members got that stamp and other people didn't.

I tell this story about my family for a few reasons. First, it's a reminder, as we follow the news about what is happening at our borders, that this is not the first time people have fled from homes in other countries, seeking to find refuge in the United States. Nor is it the first time that many Americans sought to keep those refugees out because they feared that some of those immigrants might somehow cause us harm.

But I also tell this story because that page with my grandmother's visa is a pretty sacred piece of paper for me. To state it plainly, I *do not exist without that piece of paper.* And this is a reminder of the human stakes of these debates over immigration.

And, as someone who only exists because America was a safe haven for at least some people fleeing danger and persecution, it is a reminder for me of my moral responsibilities as a citizen. It would be the height of hypocrisy if I didn't advocate for this country to remain a safe haven for that next generation of refugees.

Journey for Water

Pat Nolan

Several of us did the CROP walk last spring. The six-mile
walk is in support of people in developing countries who
typically walk at least that distance to get food, water, fuel,
or take their goods to market. It was a gorgeous day, in the
mid-50s, certainly not the hot summer day in an equatorial
country. I was armed with my water bottle. I also took a
protein bar. Well, extra sunscreen and a camera, too. I
didn't want too much to weigh me down.

During part of the walk I began to muse over how far I
would actually walk if I had to get my own daily water. If I
were adequately hydrated at the beginning, I figured I could
walk four miles and possibly six. Arriving at the source of
the water, I would wait in line, chat with the neighbors,
think of all the other things I could be doing with that time.
Then would come the walk home, carrying THE WATER.

How much could I literally carry? I envisioned myself with
a 5-gallon paint bucket. That should surely do me for a day,
or maybe longer if I dreaded the thought of tomorrow's
walk. That's about 42 pounds of water in my 5-gallon
bucket! On a good day, with just a water bottle and at my
normal hiking rate, I'd be spending two hours going to the
water source and two-plus coming back. Add the wait in
line and I've almost used up an eight-hour work day just
getting water.

Now, I am aware on an intellectual level that water is at a
premium globally. That our own Mahomet Aquifer is
beginning to be strained with the growth in population. The

United Nations High Commission for Refugees estimates that an average human needs a minimum of eight gallons of

water a day – one and a half gallons for drinking and cooking, plus six and a half gallons or more to keep clean. Right there I'm at more than a bucket and a half. The average citizen of the United States uses about 22 of my buckets every day.

But to actually walk six miles in the sandals of a woman getting her only water brings it to a more visceral level. I tried to put myself in her place on a recent walk through Meadowbrook Park. First of all, I wouldn't be wearing sandals for this walk. I need a sturdier shoe, costing many weeks of taking my produce to market.

Oh, the produce! It hasn't rained for two weeks. How much of this five gallons can I spare for my vegetables? And the baby has diarrhea again, possibly from drinking this water I'm fetching. How much can I spare to keep him clean and keep the other kids from getting sick? My daughter is home with the sick one, which means she's not with me carrying another bucket. She hasn't been to school since she was strong enough to carry water. We need more water for our family than we can haul in one trip and I must have her with me. When she isn't with me, I worry for her safety. We have to walk through some areas where the folks are not very friendly.

Oh, over there is the first blue-eyed grass I've seen in bloom this spring. I wish I could stop to admire it, but time is money and I've got to get back to tend the garden. And wash the clothes, put them out to dry. Bathe the baby how many more times today? I've been up for hours and have not yet begun the major part of the day's work.

Ok, so I obsess. But one begins to get the idea of how precious water is.

So, I begin to watch how I am using water. There are the usual culprits, showers and toilets. Cut down on that, feel better about the environment. But then there are the subtle uses which are part of the fabric of life in our developed world.

Water is used to refine oil. So, for 92 gallons of water I can drive 30 miles. With a coal-burning power plant as my power source, it costs me 14 gallons a day to have electricity.

I'm way over my five-gallon, six-mile limit.

I am humbled by that woman making her daily journey to collect water. She knows its value. May I become more aware of the living resources I often take for granted.

Cambodia 1970

Kathleen Robbins

You never know what is around the corner. I was first introduced to the UU Church when I went with my Methodist Church to El Salvador on a humanitarian service trip in 1990. Now I am a UU myself. Recently I had an experience at the annual UU General Assembly (GA) that took me back 48 years, to 1970.

There was a hint of the coming dawn over the South China Sea to the east as we began our take-off roll at Cam Ranh Bay, Vietnam. Once airborne we turned southwest and climbed to 20,000 feet. It would be a short flight, as we had a 15,000-pound bomb to drop, the largest conventional bomb in the US arsenal.

We were ordered to drop the bomb on a set of coordinates on the Vietnam/Cambodian Border in support of the impeding US incursion/invasion of Cambodia. It was May 1,1970 and President Nixon was giving a nationwide address while we were flying to our target.

My crew and I were one of five crews trained to drop these large bombs. We started out with 10,000-pound bombs left over from the Korean War; this was our first 15,000-pound bomb.

The "normal" use of the bomb was to instantly clear a helicopter landing zone in the jungle, but this was different. We were told to expect anti-aircraft fire and surface-to-air missiles, so rather than drop down from our normal altitude of 6,000 feet, we planned to climb to 20,000 feet and drop bombs from there.

Normally we would feel a small "bump" as the shock wave of the explosion hit our aircraft; this time the bomb set off a secondary explosion on the ground that was larger than that caused by the bomb we dropped. Whether that larger explosion was by coincidence or military design I will never know, but for that mission I was awarded the Distinguished Flying Cross.

With the advantage of 20/20 hindsight it is clear me that my actions and those of the entire US enterprise led to the "Killing Fields," the murder of 1.5 to 2 million Cambodians by the Khmer Rouge. No one, including Nixon and Kissinger, foresaw the horror that invasion unleashed.

I don't "blame myself," but I do recognize that my actions contributed to that holocaust and I have consequently become committed to charitable work in trouble spots of the world; trying to change the balance.

Fast-forward 48 years. I was attending the Unitarian-Universalist Service Committee (UUSC) gala, hoping to meet the person responsible for the UUSC effort in Haiti, where I currently do much of my humanitarian work. I never did meet him, but at the same affair, the Eleanor Roosevelt Humanitarian Award was presented. Past awardees include Martin Luther King III, Anita Hill, Barney Frank, and John Lewis.

This year's recipient was Loung Ung from Cambodia (born in April 1970), author of *First They Killed My Father*, a book about her family's experience during the Killing Fields.

Needless to say, her presentation was an incredibly powerful and emotional experience for me. After her speech, I went up to her to do the only thing I *could* do: apologize for my role in the Cambodian holocaust.

Fortunately, Loung was very generous and accepted my apology.

I don't have PTSD or anything like that, but I need to take responsibility for my actions and the outcomes they caused. I wonder what is around the next corner. One thing I know for sure is that we need to build a new way!

We have been at war in Afghanistan for 17 years with no end in sight; children are being separated from their parents and it goes on and on. My hope is that nobody else ever has to write a life-changing story about an experience like mine.

Insight Working

Kathleen Robinson

In 1998 I was an instructional designer for a company that created online lessons on a variety of topics for a wide range of clients. I led a design and programming team working on a series of math lessons on "Estimation" and we had devised a game-like scenario that presented a fair amount of challenge to us as creators. Our work spaces were open cubicles with walls only four feet high, making it easier for the design team to collaborate.

At noon, we usually gathered in a small kitchen to eat together and talk about one person's travel plans, another's vegetable garden. On this particular day, the people with cubicles near mine headed for the kitchen a few minutes before I did. I knew it was noon only because they distracted me slightly as they headed past my space. I was working out a tricky passage in the game's plot narrative and said I'd join them soon.

Several minutes later, clear as a bell, the voice in my head said sharply, even fiercely, *"I can't lose two children on the same date!"* I was startled. It was clearly *my* "head voice," but it seemed to have come out of nowhere.

What did I just say? What children? What date?

I glanced at the calendar and saw that it was November 30, the date when baby Emily had died more than twenty years before. Some years when I have time on my hands, I remember her and feel vaguely sad on that date, but other years it comes and goes with no special significance.

Still, what did the voice mean?

I thought of Andrew, so far away at college in Connecticut, and wondered if he were in danger. These thoughts zinged through my mind in just seconds, then faded as the memory of the voice became just that—a memory, rather than the fierce presence it had at first seemed. But my concentration was broken, so I decided to join the gang in the lunchroom.

It *had* been a disturbing occurrence, though. I began to tell my friends in the kitchen about the strange, compelling thought I'd just had. Then, as I was taking my box of dinner leftovers from the fridge, the company's office manager appeared in the kitchen doorway, breathless and looking a little wild.

"Kathy, you've got to come to the phone right away. It's Howie, he says Zak's been in an accident, but he's OK."

I dropped the plastic box that held my lunch and dashed past her, running to my cubicle, forgetting that I could have picked up the call at any of the desk phones along the way. Howie's voice was reassuring. "Zak is OK, they say, but he's at Mercy Hospital, the emergency room, being checked out. I'll meet you there. But don't rush, he really is OK."

And he *was* OK, miraculously. About a mile from my office building, riding his bicycle home from high school to fix a bowl of soup for lunch, Zak had crossed a side street without checking for traffic. He had the right of way, technically, but thick bushes along the sidewalk limited the visibility.

The driver of a white pickup truck had paused at the Stop sign, then started up again before Zak appeared in his line of sight. As the small truck's hood struck Zak's left thigh, the driver slammed on the brakes. Zak was knocked to the pavement, which he hit hard enough to crack his bike helmet. His left leg was badly bruised, and he was shaken up, but okay.

From the police report, we knew that all this happened at four minutes after noon. Only I also knew it happened several minutes after my colleagues had headed to the lunchroom on the stroke of noon, talking and laughing— just when I heard the voice in my head issue an injunction…or an angry prayer.

At night, I ponder this thing in my heart.

Summer Invasion

Umeeta Sadarangani

"I was *so* scared!" My mother shuddered.

I had asked my parents whether they were afraid during
their journey from Kuwait across the desert through Iraq to
Jordan in September of 1990, after Iraq invaded Kuwait.
My mother's prompt answer surprised me because she
rarely talks about the difficult times.

My father is the storyteller in our family, and his laughing
reply was typical of how he tries to make light of the
hardest times: "Ah, we were traveling across Iraq. Kuwait
was only one more province of Iraq. The nineteenth
province. What could they do to us?"

He was referring to Saddam Hussein's declaration claiming
Kuwait when he invaded the tiny neighboring emirate on
August 2, 1990. My parents were among more than a
quarter-million Indians who lived and worked in Kuwait,
and the Iraqi invasion displaced my parents for the second
time in their lives. The first time was in 1947, when they
were among the twelve million Indians who crossed borders
during the Partition of India, an event that has been called
the largest forced migration of people in history.

&

We were chatting about this on a summer day in 2011. My
parents were visiting my partner Marilyn and me at our
home in Champaign, Illinois, for a few weeks. Most of the
year they live in Connecticut with my younger brother,
Yogesh, and his family, and they spend a few months back
in Bombay, too. When they come to stay with us, I stock up

on some of their favorite foods. They were sitting at the kitchen counter as I brought humus for them from the fridge so they could dip pita in it. "Pitas filled with humus, cucumbers, and tomatoes make delicious sandwiches!" I told them.

"Oh, we know that," my father replied. "That was our meal in Jordan in the camp." And that was how we started talking about the summer of 1990.

My parents told me they got a meal just once a day at the refugee camp in Jordan: *khubs* (pita), cucumber, and yogurt.

"I don't know how they kept the yogurt fresh," my father mused. He is a doctor and has always thought about such details. "It was good though. We appreciated getting the food."

Just after I had received news that my parents were safely in the camps, the first news I'd had of them in the weeks since the invasion, Penn State's *Daily Collegian* had run a story about the refugee camps in Jordan.

"I was reading the newspaper in my friend Tom's apartment," I told my parents, not knowing if I had shared this memory before. "I was there to type a paper on his computer. I told Tom, 'Cucumbers and pita, that's what my parents are eating today. That's what the Red Cross is handing out.'" I remember how I had laughed then with Tom. Knowing my parents were in the camp that was described in the newspaper seemed surreal, and that was, in part, why I was laughing. Mostly, I was elated and relieved to know they were finally out of Kuwait, more than a month after the invasion began.

After the invasion and before they left Kuwait, they had begun to ration their food; friends had advised them to cook less at each meal since they could not be sure how long they would have to make the food last. When they left Kuwait, they gave most of the remaining food to their Sri Lankan maid, Chandra—after setting aside a little in their apartment in case they were turned back somewhere along the way and had to return home.

Aiming to return to Bombay, my parents and a couple of dozen Indian friends left Kuwait in a bus rented with the help of the Indian embassy. Each person could bring one suitcase. In the September heat, they made it across Iraq and into Jordan, staying in two camps along the way.

The group designated my father as their spokesperson; he dealt with the checkpoints. Indian passports marked this group as unthreatening. Unlike my parents' British friends, this group was not stopped at gunpoint and sent back to Kuwait, and unlike their American friends, these Indians were unworthy of being taken hostage.

As they waited in Amman for the flight to Bombay organized by the Indian government for Indian nationals fleeing Kuwait, they had their first hot meal in days.

"*Daal* and rice. Hot, hot." my mother recalled. "We were so happy!" I could imagine the comfort of the familiar lentil soup, a staple of the Indian diet, and it made me sad to think how much it had meant to them to have it.

"In the camps, we had to wait in line for the food. It was so hot in the sun. And first there was no food. And we were in the big shed. No rooms. We had to put our trunks to make our area. It was hell."

My mother seemed to be far away, her eyes remembering something she did not want to see. *Trunks*? A *shed*? She was thinking of 1947, I realized, when she had arrived in Bombay by ship from Karachi with her three younger siblings and their mother, my Naani. My mother had been twelve, her mother twenty-nine.

I looked at Marilyn and realized she also had noticed the shift in my mother's story—and that my mother had not. My father seemed at a loss. Marilyn and I began talking about something else—I cannot recall now what it was—and lightened the mood, moving my mother gently away from her mixed-up memories.

My mother's experience in 1990 had made her relive the trauma of 1947. Within her, the two experiences seemed intertwined, sometimes even inseparable.

&

That conversation in the kitchen took me back to the day that marks the line between "before" and "after" in my young adulthood.

On the evening of August 1, 1990, I was sitting on a bench on the mall at Penn State, a place still very new to me. I was twenty-three and had moved to State College, Pennsylvania, one month before from Boston, after receiving my master's degree in British Literature. I did not have a job yet—*could* not, as an international student who was not yet enrolled in the classes that would lead to my doctorate—so I was frugal.

That evening, I was eating hot dogs for dinner, purchased at a convenience store on College Avenue at "two for ninety-nine cents." Relish, mustard, and ketchup on one and sauerkraut on the other would balance out the meal. I was wearing a white, cotton *salwaar kameez*, north Indian baggy pants and tunic that I wore with a *dupatta*, a flowing scarf, draped over my shoulders. The air was warm, and the sun was shining through the branches of stately Dutch elms that lined the mall.

When I was single, as I was then, I often found that time of evening lonely, a time when people ought to be sitting down to dinner in warmly lit dining rooms with people who love them. It was the hardest time of day. Sitting on a bench on the mall to eat dinner made this town, where I knew very few people, where I had not yet found places to belong, a little less lonely.

After eating my dinner of hotdogs, I walked home to my studio apartment about a mile away. The apartment came with free cable, a luxury I enjoyed on the used, black and white television my brother, Yogesh, had found abandoned in his dorm in Connecticut and had given to me. I usually watched old movies on AMC, American Movie Classics. That evening, though, I was looking forward to *Nightline*. Ted Koppel was going to focus on what happened to the children of lesbians when couples split up.

I was slowly coming to terms with my attraction to women, and I wanted to learn everything I could about lesbians. So, I turned on the television at eleven-thirty that night—only to find live footage of Kuwait in the early morning, Iraqi tanks moving along familiar roads in front of the Arabian Gulf and the Hilton Hotel, not far from where I had gone to school in the late seventies and early eighties. Ted Koppel announced that the scheduled program would be preempted because Iraq had just invaded Kuwait.

I watched in disbelief until the commercial and then phoned Yogesh in Connecticut. "Turn on the TV," I said to him. "Iraq has just invaded Kuwait."

"What?" He sounded baffled. And then, a second later, "What channel?"

"ABC."

I heard him turn on the TV, heard an echo of the voice that was filling my small apartment.

Suddenly he said, "Why aren't you watching CNN? Turn it to CNN." I hadn't even thought to do that; cable was still new to me. And I liked Ted Koppel. "More people get their news from ABC News than from any other source" was what the network claimed, and I had always felt included in that number, having watched Peter Jennings and Ted Koppel since I first came to college in the US in 1984.

But I changed the channel. Yogesh and I listened and watched together, quiet in our shock. For weeks after that, my television was tuned to CNN almost nonstop. I would scold the reporters for leaving out details, for not saying from which part of Kuwait they were reporting. I needed to know so I could guess how our parents might be doing.

Yogesh and I had not been able to reach our parents by phone. By the time we tried to call, a few minutes into the news coverage that night, all the lines were already busy. And then they were cut off altogether.

The next day, I dragged myself away from the TV and walked to College Avenue in search of newspapers. At the same convenience store where I'd bought hotdogs the day before—the day before, when the world was still ordinary—I found large headlines about the invasion on the front pages of all the newspapers. I picked up the *New York Times*, the *Philadelphia Inquirer*, and the local *Centre Daily Times*.

"My parents live in Kuwait," I said to the young man behind the counter. I was trying to make a connection in a town where I knew almost no one, trying to let another human being know that my world had just been shattered. The young man looked at me blankly as he took my cash and handed me change.

I tried to comfort myself: of course, he had no response. I hadn't heard of Kuwait either, until just before we moved there when I was eleven. I left the store feeling even more alone, the newspapers heavy in my hands. Back in the apartment, I read every word, looked at the details on all the images, and continued to watch CNN.

Even now, Christiane Amanpour's name and voice bring me back to that time. She looks like my cousin Venita with her shoulder-length dark hair and striking features. She could be family. And she seemed to understand the Middle East. Christiane Amanpour became an anchor for me as I coped with the news in that sleepy college town in mid-summer.

Now, in casual conversation, when I mention my early days in the PhD program at Penn State, I sometimes tell the story of the night I learned of the invasion. I laugh a little about the *Nightline* episode on lesbians which I'd been looking forward to so eagerly. I am matter of fact about the maps of Kuwait I photocopied in Pattee Library and spread over the floor of my studio apartment.

I recount the unexpected answering machine messages from journalists and TV producers in Iraq and Jordan telling me of my parents' progress through refugee camps before they reached the Amman airport to fly to Bombay; they got my phone number from my Dad, who had thought to bring several copies of my contact information with him, hoping to meet some American journalists who could get word to me and my brother in the U.S.

As I tell these stories, I don't let myself feel the sobs that wracked me as I wondered how my mother was doing alone at home, if my father still went to work. I don't tell others what I wondered: Were soldiers patrolling the complex where they lived? Did they have electricity in the desert summer? Did they have water and food? Would I see them again?

&

All these decades later, when I watch the evening news and see refugees waiting at borders or hear them speaking of homes they have left behind, when I encounter international students in the US affected by political upheaval, their uncertainties feel familiar, and that summer of the Iraqi invasion becomes vivid again.

Safari

Sarah Wisseman

Nairobi, Kenya. February, 2001

A week after the accident, I found myself alone for the first time. My husband was still in hospital and young Andrew had just departed for Boston with his grandmother. I'd been warned not to wander around the city by myself—unless I took off my watch and my wedding ring and carried no more cash than I could afford to lose. But I thought I could make it across the street from my hotel to the enormous, open air Catholic cathedral for the English service.

I entered the building, marveling at the arches open to the sky and the birds flying in and out. Soon I found myself in a long pew, shoulder to shoulder with strangers. Although I was nearly the only white person in a cathedral that seated thousands, I did not feel unwelcome. Instead, I felt safe— safe enough to let go and cry for the first time.

❧

Charlie and I had signed up for an African safari, a fifteen-day trip to celebrate our 25th wedding anniversary. We traveled in a Land Rover with four other passengers and our genial Kenyan driver, Godfrey. After several days of alternately teasing and grousing at each other and choosing the same seats in the van each morning, we became an odd sort of family.

Bouncy, talkative Andrew sat next to me. Behind us were Andrew's intrepid Greek grandmother, Vangi, who'd promised to take her grandson to Africa to see the animals when he turned twelve, and Marta. Marta, an elderly and introverted Argentinian, was the subject of much grousing—she made the rest of us wait at every stop while she took just one more photograph with her fancy camera. John, a pleasant single man from New York City, sat in back with my husband Charlie.

We became experienced in the requirements of a safari, such as the need for an iron bladder and consequent reduction of morning caffeine. "No, you may not get out of the vehicle to go to the bathroom whenever you feel the need," said Godfrey. "See that lioness sticking her head up from the tall grasses?" He also warned us to "guard your food" at one of our lunch stops, but we didn't understand. Charlie opened his lunch box and bit into a chicken leg. The next moment, a dive-bombing kite snatched the food from his hand.

We learned about elephants. "When the bull elephant flaps his ears, he is getting angry." When this happened to us, Godfrey yelled "Aiee!" and threw the truck into reverse with indecent speed. At another stop, the crude outhouse bore a sign: "Restroom Closed due to Elephants." Nearby, a large elephant regarded us blandly. *Tough luck, tourists!*

On Day Five, we drove into the Serengeti of Tanzania, a vast savanna covered with grasses and migrating wildebeest. We were traveling on one of the best unpaved roads of the entire trip, flat and relatively wide, when the right rear tire exploded. The Land Rover bucked and swayed, rolling into a ditch and onto its roof.

The crash itself was eerily silent. It was only when the vehicle came to rest that sounds returned: groans and yelps of pain as people rose from the wreckage, Godfrey calling for help on the radio, the sudden babel of Japanese as a carload of medics arrived.

Charlie, Vangi, and Marta were knocked unconscious. Godfrey suffered a broken arm. Andrew and I were uninjured—Andrew because he had the good sense to wrap his arms around the seat in front of him when he felt the vehicle roll, me because I'd earlier found an ancient seat belt wrapped around my seat and put it on.

Everyone survived except John, who was thrown out of the open roof and killed instantly. The rest of us were taken to a field station where Charlie's flesh wound was wrapped and Vangi and Marta had their neck injuries examined. As we waited in a Flying Doctor's plane, Charlie said he felt faint. He became pale and silent. I worried about internal injuries until the pilot gave me something else to think about: we had to leave soon before the light faded in order to navigate over the Great Rift Valley back to Nairobi.

At the hospital, the doctor told us Charlie had eight broken ribs and an air leak—a lung puncture—that would keep him in the hospital. Vangi was also hospitalized, so Andrew became my new roommate. After I spoke with Andrew's parents in Boston by telephone, we were driven to the hotel that became my home for the next three weeks. It was midnight, and we had not eaten since lunchtime.

I made Andrew drink a couple of glasses of water. I drank some too, since I knew we were both dehydrated. As he curled up in his bed, the bubble of numbness that had shielded me so far began to crack. I whispered the Lord's Prayer over and over until I was able to sleep.

When we returned to the hospital the next day, I felt another quiver of fear when I discovered Charlie had been moved— to the High Dependency Unit. Surprise: the HDU stood open to the outside air and insects, as well as relatives parading through to the waiting room—a porch on the far side of the ward. To my relief, Charlie was alert and sitting up, despite numerous tubes connecting him to machines.

The next week was a blur of hospital visits and taking care of Andrew. I played assistant nurse and helped Charlie take his first shower when it was clear the nurses were way too busy. We learned that our hospital was the second best on the continent of Africa, but most Kenyans could not afford the fee of one dollar per day. Charlie discovered that the kerosene lanterns in each room were not just decorative; they were used daily whenever the power went out.

He felt like he'd time-traveled back to the 1950s, a patient in a hospital where nurses still took armpit temperatures and refused to give him pain medication: "Why do you need it? You are walking around." Not only did Charlie's bed have an enormous mosquito net hanging over it, but the water pitcher had a cute little mosquito net too.

The tour company asked me to talk with John's sister by long-distance telephone to explain what had happened to her brother. I was haunted by the fact that John had died but Charlie had lived—all because the two men had changed places in the safari vehicle on the morning of the crash. One of our fellow tourists (Marta) wanted to blame the driver for negligent driving, but I testified to the police that the crash was not Godfrey's fault; it was merely an accident that could have happened anywhere.

Andrew, a charming and loyal kid who reminded me of my own son, kept me from falling apart. Once he got over being scared about his grandmother, he asked me shyly, "Do you think the hotel…could the hotel make me a cheese pizza?"

They could—and did. In fact, the two of us were treated like honored guests by the hotel staff: "How is your husband today, Mrs. Wisseman? Andrew, how is your grandmother?" One shopkeeper gave me a little ebony wood rhinoceros as a farewell gift; it is one of my most treasured keepsakes.

Charlie was released from the hospital after eight days, but we couldn't fly home for another two weeks until his lung puncture healed. That was okay with me. When I looked at the map of Africa with countries we would fly over—Uganda, the Congo—emergency landing, anyone? No thanks.

While we waited, we had several small adventures that never would have happened as part of our regular tour. John's aunt Victoria, who lived in Nairobi because her husband worked for USAID, invited us to dinner in her comfortable home inside an armed compound topped with razor wire. Her husband described how difficult it was to funnel American money into the hands of people who really needed it instead of the pockets of corrupt officials.

Traveling around Nairobi, we saw streets with truck-sized potholes, streets that hadn't been repaired since the British left. While we enjoyed an English-style tea at the hotel, the local paper informed us that the sales of machetes had ticked up because of an impending election. In the same paper, we read of the high percentage of HIV in the local blood supply and felt grateful Charlie had not needed a transfusion.

Leah, the kind woman assigned to us after the accident by the local tour company, continued to visit us. She and her driver would just show up at the hotel because she knew only too well that the local telephone system was abysmal.

When my prescriptions ran out, she took me to a pharmacy where I could buy them over the counter, at a fraction of the prices I paid back in Illinois.

Other memories from that bittersweet time: Returning to the Catholic cathedral with Charlie, sitting in packed pews and listening to African chanted hymns and watching pigeons flying around near the ceiling. Staying in touch with Godfrey, our safari driver, who worried about the survival of his job and his ability to pay for the education of his four children. Shopping with Victoria at an open-air market: someone wanted to buy my sweaty sun visor because he'd never seen such a thing before.

Another man gave me a skin drum in exchange for a ballpoint pen. Visiting a giraffe sanctuary: we joined other tourists climbing stairs up to a platform at giraffe head level. We bought giraffe food and marveled at the long, black, slimy tongues as the giraffes ate from our hands.

When we flew home, almost a month after the accident, Charlie still suffered from a persistent cough that made him feel like he was being stabbed with knives because of the broken ribs. As we approached Chicago, the sight of the familiar flat terrain brought tears to my eyes. After we finally pulled into our own driveway, Charlie hauled himself out of the van, knelt, and kissed the driveway.

We were greeted by our orange cat Tigger, who'd been injured while we were away. Wearing a purple bandage around his tummy, the cat slept on Charlie's chest whenever he could, snuggled close to Charlie's blue arm sling. Two old friends recovering together from the wars.

☟

Champaign, February 2019

There is nothing like a near-death experience to sharpen your focus and make you think about what you really want to do with the time you have left. Charlie left medicine early to become a full-time mixed media artist. I finished my first novel (the one in progress when we went to Africa) and have written and published several more mysteries. I retired from the university in 2013 to allow more time for writing, painting, and grandchildren.

This past December, I suffered a second wakeup call: a mild heart attack and a four-day hospital stay. When the angiogram revealed two almost totally blocked arteries (99% and 92%), the doctors placed two stents in my heart. I missed being a bypass case by a whisker.

Now I'm home with a slew of new medications and the realization that I've been given the second chance my mother never had (she died of a massive heart attack in 1995, at the same age I am now). As I adjust to the new reality of being a cardiac patient with some limitations, I recall what Charlie said after we came back from Kenya and many times since: "Just walking around, breathing in and out, is an underrated pleasure."

That's worth remembering.

Author Biographies

Sally (Sarah) Babbitt was born in Peoria and lived there until she graduated from the Methodist Hospital School of Nursing in 1957. She also holds a University of Illinois nursing degree. Sally followed this nursing career route for the next 25 years: Chicago, Texas, Washington DC, Maryland, New Jersey, and back to Illinois. After attending a Christmas Eve ceremony with her family at UUC Urbana, she felt so warmly welcomed by open arms, she still recalls that night. "Listening to Will Sanders' voice in the dark sanctuary as candles glowed around me made me realize that this was the place I needed to be."

&

Originally from New England, **Kate Barton** moved to Illinois in 1994. She worked as the CEO of a public housing agency and affordable housing development group for 20 years and retired in 2014. Kate moved to Urbana in the Fall of 2017 after the death of her partner Monty and is enjoying life in her new home here. The quote at the beginning of Kate's story describes the first day she and Monty met.

Jerry Carden, raised as a middle-of-the-road Methodist on an Iowa farm, was traumatized by his growing attraction to men while growing up. Jerry identifies as bisexual. His relationship with husband Tim Temple began in 1981. The two became regulars at the UU Church of Urbana-Champaign in 1996 and they were married in 2004 by Rev. Keith Kron at the Unitarian Universalist Association Headquarters in Boston. Jerry retired in 2015 from a career in health care/human resource education and health behavior coaching. His BS Ed degree was in health education/biology and he later received a master's degree in adult education.

⅋

Beth Cobb was born in Champaign, Illinois in 1954. She attended Urbana public schools, University High School (class of 1971), and graduated from the U of I College of Education in 1975. Beth married Emil in 1976, and they have a son, a daughter, and a grandson. As a second-generation member of UUCUC, she has served in a great number of volunteer positions, as well as Director of Religious Education for six years in the late 1970s and early 1980s. Beth enjoys her retirement from the University of Illinois College of Law, where she worked with students who edited the law journals for 35 years. She also recently retired from UUCUC.

Gail Cohen was born in New York City, took the Jewish migration route to Miami as a pre-teen, and landed by accident in Illinois nearly 40 years ago after finishing a graduate degree in anthropology. She has enjoyed the career of her dreams as a journalist, writer, teacher, author, and giftware designer. Mom to two, grandmother to four, and great-grandmother to seven (at last count), Cohen has outlasted 3 literary agents and 3 husbands. Her goal is to keep writing until the day she's found slumped over her keyboard, with or without a cat in her arms.

&

Nancy Dietrich is a central Illinois native. She grew up in Harristown, a small town outside of Decatur, attended the University of Illinois, and got her first job out of college in Danville, where she met her (now) husband, Russ Rybicki. They moved to Urbana, where they currently reside, in 1997, the year they were married. Nancy has written many letters to the editor, articles, and op-eds over the years, including an op-ed about saving Social Security and Medicare that ran in the *Chicago Sun-Times*. This is the first time she has written about her personal life.

Lee Doppelt, a Chicago-area native who writes under several names, is a retired occupational therapist, accountant, public speaker, and teacher with a business background, who stumbled into the life of magazine writing unexpectedly, writing regularly for *The Dollar Stretcher* (www.stretcher.com), *Advance for Occupational Therapy Practitioners*, and travel articles for the *Champaign-Urbana News-Gazette*, *Prime Life Times,* and other specialty publications. Lee *also* has taught creative writing classes to children. A mother and grandmother, her interests include swimming, genealogy, listening to classical music, and playing Mahjong. She has written a novella, *Mr. America Mirage,* which can be found online. Learn more at http://debrakarplus.blogspot.com.

&

Ben Leff grew up in the Unitarian-Universalist Church of Urbana-Champaign, returning to the church a few years ago with his wife, Melissa Schoeplein, and son, Theodore Schoeplein-Leff. Ben's parents (Mark and Carol) started attending UU churches in Boston and Chicago in the 1970s. Ben's heritage is both Christian and Jewish; three-quarters of his family immigrated to the United States in the first half of the 20th century. He is currently a history teacher at University Laboratory High School and lives in Urbana.

As a child and a military dependent, **Pat Nolan** moved around frequently. A few early years were spent in Japan, which helped to form Pat's interest in other cultures. Perhaps as a result of this, she developed a sensitivity to the Newcomer in many settings. When she reached her early 50s, her goal was to fine-tune her life, realizing that the spiritual realm was one area which was lacking. Based upon the living example of a social activist Unitarian couple she knew in her 20s, Nolan tried the UU Church first. "Still here!" she adds.

&

In her "old life," **Kathleen Robbins** graduated from the Air Force Academy, flew combat missions in Vietnam and had a beautiful wife and son. When her wife died and her son went to college, she transitioned in 1990 and never looked back. Over the past 28 years, Kathleen was CEO of a small cell phone company, completed a Doctor of Ministry degree, served in the Peace Corps in Botswana, and co-founded an economic development program in Haiti. Once the executive director of a small nonprofit, she retired at the end of 2016. Kathleen "discovered" the Champaign-Urbana UU Church in 1990, becoming an official member in 1996.

Kathy (Kathleen) Robinson recently returned to poetry and short stories after a long career spent writing and editing for technical and scientific groups, a national organization of English teachers, and a Boston-based college textbook publisher. Her poems are reveries on community, family life and gardening, Kathy is a spatial designer, inserting beauty and flow into interior and garden "rooms." She is an optimist, seeing the best in everyone and everything. Kathy and her husband Howie live in Champaign-Urbana and are very involved in OLLI (Osher Lifelong Learning Institute) classes, as well as the CU Archaeology Club.

☙

Umeeta Sadarangani is a Professor of English at Parkland College in Champaign, Illinois, where she teaches writing, literature, and a humanities course on South Asian cultures. Umeeta's writing and visual art are informed by her experiences growing up in India and Kuwait, coming out as a lesbian during graduate school, and navigating the immigrant experience in the United States. Her previous publications have been in academic journals such as *American Studies International* and *Modern Language Studies* (*MLS*) and the literary journal *Bluestem*. You can find more of Umeeta's writing on her blog, *Transplanted on the Prairie* (transplantedontheprairie.blogspot.com). She has been a grateful member of UUCUC since 2001.

Sarah Wisseman, formerly an archaeological scientist at the University of Illinois, teaches archaeology, ancient technologies, and scientific detection of art forgery at the Osher Lifelong Learning Institute in Champaign. She is also a mystery author and painter (sarahwisseman.com). Her archaeological and art historical mysteries are based in places where she has lived and traveled (Massachusetts, Illinois, Israel, Italy, and Egypt), and her paintings include landscapes, seascapes, and galaxies. She lives with her husband Charlie, former pathologist and mixed-media artist (charleswisseman.com). They have two children and (soon-to-be) three grandchildren.

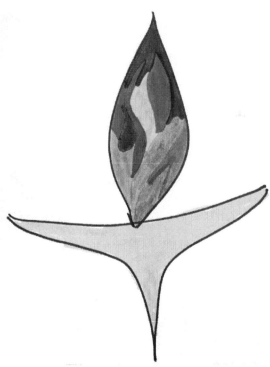

Original art drawn by Umeeta Sadarangani

Made in the USA
San Bernardino, CA
25 July 2019